Cambridge English Readers
....

Level 1

Series editor: Philip Prowse

Don't Stop Now!

Philip Prowse

CAMBRIDGE UNIVERSITY PRESS

Cambridge, New York, Melbourne, Madrid, Cape Town, Singapore, São Paulo

Cambridge University Press
The Edinburgh Building, Cambridge CB2 2RU, UK

www.cambridge.org
Information on this title: www.cambridge.org/9780521605649

First published 2005
3rd printing 2006

Philip Prowse has asserted his right to be identified as the Author
of the Work in accordance with the Copyright, Design and Patents Act 1988.

Printed in India by Thomson Press (India) Limited

Illustrations by Paul Dickinson

A catalogue record of this book is available from the British Library.

ISBN-13 978-0-521-60564-9 paperback
ISBN-10 0-521-60564-4 paperback

ISBN-13 978-0-521-60565-6 cassette
ISBN-10 0-521-60565-2 cassette

Contents

People in the story

Hi. I'm Matt. I work in London and take drinks to shops and cafés. Here are the people in the story.

This is Paolo Debono. He has a café in Soho: the Web Café.

Here's Paolo's daughter, Katerina. We call her Kate.

And then of course there are the Vassallo brothers, Antonio and Victor. But you're going to meet them later . . .

Places in the story

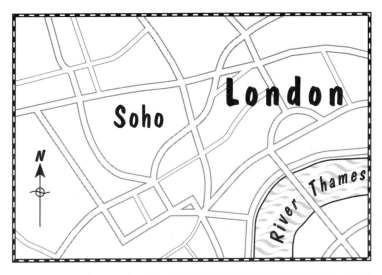

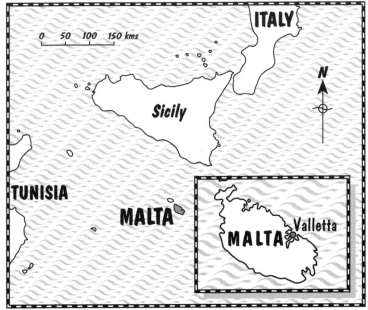

Chapter 1 *Crash!*

'Crash!'

  'Aaah!'

   I looked up from my coffee. 'Crash!' – that was the café window. And 'Aaah!' – that was Kate.

People in the café shouted. Kate and I ran to the window. There was no one there. Then I turned to Kate and put my arm around her.

'Are you all right?' I asked.

'Yes,' she said. 'I think so.'

'What is it?' someone shouted and a short red-faced man ran into the room. The man took my arm. 'Matt! What are you doing to Kate?' he asked.

'Nothing, Papa,' Kate replied. 'It wasn't him. It was from out in the street.'

The red-faced man looked at the window and then at me. He turned to his daughter.

'Are you OK, Kate?' he asked.

Kate gave him a little smile. 'Yes, I think I am, Papa,' she said.

Then her father spoke to me. 'Sorry, Matt. I heard Kate and I thought . . . '

'That's OK, Paolo,' I answered.

It was OK. You see, this is Soho, in the centre of London. In the day it's famous for music and films. At night people come and eat in the restaurants. Expensive restaurants and cheap restaurants; Italian restaurants and Chinese restaurants. And day and night there are internet cafés like the Web Café.

In Soho you can buy anything and anyone. There are lots of nice people in Soho. But there are also lots of people who are – what can I say? – not very nice. I know because I live and work here. I take drinks to the shops and cafés. I do judo most evenings and I'm good at it. I'm not rich and famous. And I don't know a lot. But I do know Soho.

I also know Paolo and the Web Café well. I often have

my morning coffee there. Paolo comes from Valletta in Malta, and he does everything in the café. He makes the coffee and other drinks at the bar, and cooks the food in the kitchen. It isn't bad food. He makes very good pizza. Maltese pizza? I know – don't ask me why. I don't eat a lot of pizza. But people do. They telephone, Paolo makes the pizzas and a boy takes the pizzas to their house. Takeaway Maltese pizza. Why not?

And why is it the Web Café and not the Pizza Café or Café Malta? Because in the café there are computers. People come to the café to use email and the internet. Lots of foreign tourists, not only Europeans, but also Americans and Japanese, come to the café to use the computers.

Kate is Paolo's daughter. She's a student, but she helps him in the café. She's why I go there a lot. Not for the coffee. Not for the pizza. Not for the computers. But for Kate. I love her brown eyes and her smile.

But Kate wasn't smiling now. She walked over to her father and took his hand.

'Was it those men?' she asked.

Paolo answered slowly, 'Yes, I think it was.'

I looked at the father and daughter. I didn't understand. Who were 'those men'?

Chapter 2 *Don't stop now!*

I saw a small piece of paper near the window. There was writing on the paper, but I didn't understand it. The writing wasn't in English. I gave the paper to Paolo. He read it slowly.

'What does it say?' I asked.

'It's in Maltese,' Paolo answered.

'Who is it from?' I asked. 'And the window? Why?'

Paolo didn't say anything. He just looked at the paper.

'Come on, Paolo,' I said. 'You know me. You can tell me.'

Paolo looked up at me. 'Yes,' he answered. 'You are a friend, but you are not in our family. There is nothing I can say – you understand? Now I must get a new window.'

Paolo walked to the telephone at the back of the café. I turned to Kate. 'Well?' I asked. 'What's it all about?'

Kate looked quickly back at her father. 'Not now,' she said. 'Come back later. Then we can talk.'

'OK,' I smiled. 'Anyway, I must get back to work. See you later.' I left the café and walked across the road to my lorry.

I finished work at seven in the evening and went back to the Web Café. It was always good to talk to Kate, but today I wanted answers to some questions.

'Why?' I asked Kate when I sat down at the bar. 'Why your window? Who are "those men"? What do they want?'

'Questions, questions. You ask a lot of questions.' Kate gave me a little smile. 'Just like the police.'

Now I smiled. 'You know me, Kate,' I said. 'I'm a driver, not the police.'

People often find it easy to talk to me. Everyone, not just my friends. Well, not my family. My mother and father are dead, and I don't have any brothers or sisters. I don't have a wife – sometimes there's a girl, but only for a short time.

A girl friend, not a girlfriend, actually, if you understand me. I'm 20, and I love football and judo. I also love Kate, but she doesn't know that.

I waited while two American tourists paid to use the computers with their credit cards. Kate put their cards through the credit card machine.

'It's not easy for Papa,' Kate said. She looked quickly to the back of the café, but her father was in the kitchen. 'He works and works all day. And now there's this.'

Kate had the piece of paper in her hand. She read it again.

'What does it say?' I asked.

Kate looked around again. No Paolo. 'It's in Maltese. It says "Don't stop now!"'

'Who wrote this?' I asked.

'One of two men – I don't know which,' Kate said. 'I think my father knew them in Malta a long time ago. The two men from Malta came here eight weeks ago and talked to my father. After they left, Papa wasn't happy. But he didn't tell me what the men wanted.'

'Did the men come back?' I asked.

'Yes,' Kate answered. 'The next day. They brought all these new computers.'

'Oh?' I said. 'Was your father happy then?'

'No . . .' Kate looked up and stopped. Paolo was at the kitchen door. He had the phone in his hand.

'What is it, Papa?' Kate asked.

'It's Bob – the boy who takes our pizzas to people. He doesn't want to work for us now,' Paolo said.

'Why not?' Kate asked.

'He knows about the window. And one of our "friends" went to see him. Now Bob's afraid to work for me. What are we going to do?' Paolo replied.

Kate thought for a minute and then she smiled. 'I know, Papa,' she said. 'I can take the pizzas.'

Paolo closed his eyes. 'No, no, no. Never. You're my only daughter. And these men . . .'

'Papa,' Kate said with a smile. She put her arm around her father. 'It's OK. I'm a big girl now. I want to help.'

Paolo looked at Kate. 'No, my love. I'm afraid for you. I don't want you to . . .'

'You mustn't be afraid. And anyway . . .' Kate's brown eyes turned to me, 'Matt's going to come with me.'

My mouth opened. It was one of my judo nights.

Chapter 3 *The 'special' pizza*

'I'm going to do what?' I asked.

Kate took my hand and smiled. 'Please, help me with the pizzas.' I looked into her beautiful brown eyes. 'OK,' I said. 'But when?'

'Now,' Kate answered. 'All right, Papa?'

Paolo smiled. 'All right,' he said. 'Thank you Matt – you're a good friend. Oh, and there's also a "special" pizza, Kate. You know what to do.'

Kate looked at her father. 'I understand,' she said.

Paolo went back into the kitchen.

I didn't understand. 'What's special about the "special" pizza?' I asked.

'You ask too many questions,' Kate replied with a black look.

Then Paolo came out of the kitchen with boxes of pizzas.

'Now you drive slowly,' Paolo said to his daughter and gave her a kiss.

'Yes, Papa,' Kate said.

Five minutes later Kate and I were on the motorbike. We had helmets on and the pizzas were in a box on the back of the motorbike. Kate knew where to take the pizzas. And I knew where to put my hands – around Kate!

Kate started the motorbike and we drove off. The motorbike went very fast in and out of the cars.

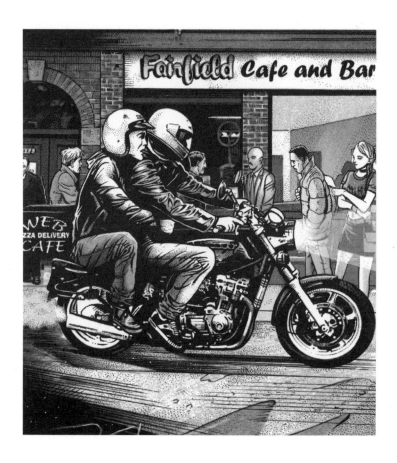

'Slow down!' I said in Kate's ear, but she didn't listen. 'Please!' I said again. 'I'm too young to die!'

Kate looked back at me, but she didn't smile. We got to the first house. Kate went to the door and a woman opened it. Kate gave her a pizza and came back to the motorbike with the money. On to the next house, and the next. Sometimes houses, sometimes flats. I waited with the motorbike and Kate took the pizzas. Then she drove fast to the next house. Kate stopped and took a pizza to the door.

I looked at my watch. Eight o'clock. I was hungry. I looked around, but I couldn't see Kate. I opened the box on the motorbike. There was only one pizza in it. It was the 'special' pizza. What was a 'special' pizza anyway? I quickly opened the 'special' pizza box. But there was no pizza in it, only a small black box. What was that box? I half-remembered seeing something like it. But where?

I heard a noise and turned around. It was Kate. I closed the 'special' pizza box and put it back.

Kate came back to the motorbike. She had that black look on her face again. 'OK,' she said. 'One more pizza and then we can go back to the café.'

I didn't say anything. We got on and Kate started the motorbike.

'Are you all right?' I asked. 'You don't look very happy.'

'Sorry,' she answered. 'I'm thinking.'

'About what?' I asked.

'Something to eat,' she replied.

'I'm hungry too,' I said.

'We can eat when we get back to the café,' Kate replied.

I wanted to ask Kate about the 'special' pizza, but she started to drive fast. I put my arms around her quickly. Kate drove on and then stopped outside an office. She got off the motorbike and took off her helmet. She opened the box and took out the last pizza box. Her brown eyes looked sad and angry.

'Are you all right?' I asked again. 'I can take the pizza.'

'No, it's OK,' she replied. 'I'm just a little tired. Please, wait here for me.'

Kate walked to the door. She waited for a minute and then the door opened. But this time she went in.

I sat on the motorbike and thought, 'Kate isn't happy.' She didn't want to go to the office. Why? And what was the small black box? I waited five minutes. No Kate. I waited. No Kate. Where was she?

I got off the motorbike and started to walk to the office door. Just then Kate came out. She had the pizza box under her arm. She wasn't smiling. A man in a long coat closed the door behind her.

'OK?' I asked.

'Yes,' she answered. Her head was down. She put on her helmet, put the pizza box back and got on the motorbike. 'But they didn't want the pizza. It was cold. Come on. We're going back to the café.'

We left the motorbike outside the café and went in. It was dark and there was no one there.

'Hi, Paolo!' I said. 'We're back!'

Kate put the pizza box on the bar. 'Papa's in the kitchen,' she said and went to the back of the café.

I looked at the pizza box on the bar. 'Why not have a look?' I thought. There was no one in the dark café. I looked around, then opened the box quickly. No change. A small black box. Was it the old box or a new one? I didn't know. I closed the pizza box and put it back on the bar.

Then I walked to the back of the café. I opened the kitchen door and saw Paolo's back. He was on the phone. Kate was there. Her face was white and she was very afraid.

'No! No! No!' Paolo shouted into the phone.

Chapter 4   *The Kiss of Death*

'No!' Paolo shouted into the phone again and put it down on a table. Then he turned and saw me. His face was red and angry.

'What's wrong, Papa?' Kate asked.

'Things are very, very bad,' Paolo replied. 'And where's the box?'

'It's on the bar,' I said. 'Can I help?'

'Matt,' Paolo shouted, 'this is nothing to do with you. You are a good friend. But this is about our family and you are not in our family.' He was still very angry.

'Don't speak to Matt like that, Papa,' Kate said. 'He was very kind and went with me on the motorbike.'

'I'm sorry, Matt,' Paolo said. 'Thank you very much for your help tonight. But you can't help any more.'

Kate put her hand on my arm. 'I think it's time for you to go now, Matt. I'm very sorry.'

I said good night and left the kitchen. Kate walked with me through the café. 'I'm sorry about my father . . .' she started.

'That's OK,' I replied. 'I can see that he's very angry. I'm working late tomorrow. I'm afraid I can't help with the pizzas.'

'Come and see me tomorrow evening at nine – when I get back here,' Kate said. 'We can talk then. And again, thank you for all your help.'

I smiled. 'See you at nine,' I answered. As I left the café,

Kate went behind the bar and got the 'special' pizza box.

The next evening at nine I left my lorry outside the Web Café. There were only two or three people there, sitting at the computers. Paolo was behind the bar. A woman came up and paid with a credit card to use a computer. I waited and then walked to the bar.

Paolo's face was white and his eyes were red.

'Hello, Matt,' Paolo said slowly. He stopped and looked up and down the bar. There was no one there. He came near me. 'I'm very sorry about yesterday. I shouted at you . . . I know you wanted to help.'

I smiled and waited. 'Is Kate still out with the pizzas?' I asked.

'Yes, she is. Kate and I talked about things last night and I want to talk to you now,' Paolo said. 'I want to tell you about two men who came to see us – two men from Malta: Antonio and Victor Vassallo. They're men I knew years ago – when I lived in Valletta. They're "businessmen" and their business is money.'

'I see,' I said. But I didn't.

'Two months ago they came to see me here,' Paolo said. 'First they gave me all these new computers. Then they asked me to "help" them for two or three weeks.'

'"Help" them? Help them do what?' I asked.

'Something very easy,' Paolo replied. 'All I did was put a small black box on the bar by the credit card machine. Every evening I gave them the box and they gave me a new box.'

'What does the black box do?' I asked.

'Something to do with credit card numbers,' Paolo said.

'Now I understand,' I said after thinking for a minute.

19

'The Vassallo brothers are taking the credit card numbers of people who use your café.'

'But why?' Paolo asked.

'I think I know why,' I replied. 'And when did these black boxes start?'

'I "helped" the Vassallo brothers for three weeks, and then for three more weeks,' Paolo answered. 'I tried to stop, but it was always "only two or three days". And then last night I said again, "Stop! I'm going to the police!"'

'And . . .?' I asked

'This evening the Vassallo brothers came here when there was no one in the café,' Paolo replied. 'They gave me the "Kiss of Death".'

'What's that?' I asked.

'In Malta,' Paolo said, 'when you give someone the "Kiss of Death" you are telling them, "Do what we say or someone in your family is going to die."'

Just then we heard the motorbike.

'Oh!' Paolo said with a quick smile. 'That's Kate! She's back!'

Paolo ran to the door. But when the door opened, a tall man in a long coat stood there.

'Your motorbike is here, Paolo,' the man said with a cold smile. 'But we've got your daughter. Now do what we say! One more day. Tomorrow you can have your daughter and we go back to Malta.'

Chapter 5 *Everything went black*

The tall man walked into the café and went up to the bar. I turned and sat down at one of the computers. My back was to the bar, but I heard what the tall man said to Paolo.

'Here are your motorbike keys and here's a new box. Put it by the machine now. Give it to us tomorrow night and you can have your daughter.'

'Where is she? Where's Kate?' Paolo asked.

'She's OK,' the man said. 'She's with Victor. He likes her.' The man smiled that cold smile again and left the café. Paolo closed the door behind him. His face was white.

I got up from the computer and went over to the bar. Paolo looked at me. He had the small black box in his hand. Then he put it on the bar by the credit card machine.

'What are you doing?' I asked.

'I'm doing what Antonio Vassallo asked,' Paolo replied. 'I want to see Kate again.'

'You're going to see her tonight, not tomorrow,' I said. The motorbike keys were now in my hand.

'What are *you* doing?' Paolo asked.

'I know where they've got Kate,' I answered. 'I'm going to go there now before Antonio gets back. And before Victor does anything to Kate.'

Paolo opened his mouth to reply. But I ran out of the café and got on the motorbike. I drove fast through Soho. I knew where Kate was – at the office where she took the 'special' pizza. I left the motorbike 100 metres from the office and walked down the dark street.

When I got to the office I saw that there was a light on. Outside in the street it was very dark. There were some trees by the door and I stood behind them and waited. I listened but there were no noises from the office or the street. Five minutes. Ten minutes. Then I heard someone. Someone walking down the street.

It was Antonio. He stopped in front of the office and took out a key. Then he opened the door. I started to come out from behind the trees, but I made a noise. Antonio stopped and looked around. Then he walked over to the trees. I waited. 'What can I do?' I thought. Antonio was

very near. I looked down at my hands. The motorbike
helmet!

I ran out from the trees. 'Crash!' That was the
motorbike helmet on Antonio's head. 'Aaaah!' That was
Antonio. Then I used my judo. One minute later Antonio
was on the ground.

'Who's that?' someone shouted.

'It must be Victor,' I thought. I went back behind the
trees.

Victor came to the door. He had a gun in his hand. He
looked around and then saw Antonio on the ground.
Victor went down on his knees by his brother. When I ran
out Victor looked up at me. More judo and Victor's gun
was in my right hand.

Leaving Antonio outside, I took Victor back into the
office.

'Matt!' It was Kate. She was in a chair and there were ropes around her legs. There were two beds in the room and a table and chairs. On the table there was some old food, some machines and lots of credit cards.

I took Victor over to Kate. 'Help her!' I said.

Victor started to take off the ropes. Kate looked at me and smiled. Then she stopped smiling and looked behind me. What did she see? And why did she stop smiling?

I turned my head and understood. It was Antonio. Then everything went black.

Chapter 6 *Don't use the gun!*

'You! Who are you?!' someone shouted. It was a man.

I opened my eyes. It was Antonio. He was angry and he had Victor's gun in his hand.

'Who are you? Police?' Antonio shouted again and pointed the gun at me.

'Talk or die!' Antonio shouted with the gun in his hand.

'Stop! He isn't the police. He's my friend.' It was Kate. She was behind me.

'Antonio!' Victor shouted. 'Stop asking questions and come and help me.' Victor took the credit cards from the table and put them into a bag. 'These two are going to die anyway.'

Antonio laughed and went over to help his brother.

'Are you OK?' Kate asked.

'I think I am,' I replied. Then I shouted to the brothers, 'Hey, you two! Kate can go. She doesn't know anything.'

'Oh yes she does.' Antonio turned to us with his cold smile. 'You know everything, my little Kate, don't you?' He walked over and put his hand on her hair. 'Now, Kate, why don't you tell your friend what we are doing?'

'I . . . I . . .' Kate started and then stopped.

'Go on, Kate,' Antonio said coming over to me. The gun was in his hand. 'Or your friend . . .'

'This is what I think,' I said before Kate started. 'It's about credit cards and money. The black box by the credit card machine in the Web Café takes the numbers of the credit cards.'

'Yes, and every night we bring the black box here and get a new one,' Kate said. 'Then Victor makes new credit cards with the numbers.'

'Mm. Good! But not all the numbers, my little Kate,' Antonio said. 'Just the numbers from foreign tourists' credit cards. And then what do we do, Kate?'

'I don't know,' Kate replied.

'I think I do,' I said. 'The cards go to other countries.'

'Very good, Mr . . . What's your name?' Antonio asked.

'Matt.'

'Yes, Mr Matt. It's very easy – like taking money from a baby,' Antonio laughed. 'We give the cards to our friends in Malta, in New York, in Moscow, in Sicily, in Mexico – everywhere. And our friends only use the cards once – to take out $1,000.'

'Kate,' I asked, 'how many foreign tourists use credit

cards every day in the Web Café?'

'I don't know – 50?' she answered.

'Wow! That's 50 times $1,000 – that's $50,000 a day!' I said. 'Seven days a week for eight weeks!'

'Very good, my friend,' Antonio said. 'And that's why we are stopping now. Before the police come.'

'And before too many tourists find they have no money when they go back to their countries,' I said.

'Come on!' Victor shouted to Antonio. 'Stop talking. Time to go!'

Victor took a bottle, opened it and poured something all over the table and the machines. Then he took out a cigarette lighter and started a fire.

'Crash! Crash!'

That was my lorry when it hit the window and came into the office. Paolo was at the wheel.

'Aaah! Aaah!'

That was Antonio as the lorry hit him in the back.

'Aaah!'

That was Paolo as his head hit the wheel and the lorry stopped. Paolo's eyes closed. I looked at Antonio on the floor and saw that his eyes weren't open.

But Victor's eyes were open. He ran up to Antonio and took the gun. He looked up at Paolo in the lorry. 'Thanks, old man,' he said and laughed. 'Now I've got all the money!'

Then Victor turned to Kate and me. 'I'm going to finish you two now,' he said. He put the gun to my head.

I looked up at the gun. Then behind Victor I saw Paolo. He was out of the lorry and he had a soft drinks bottle in his hand.

'Please don't use the gun!' Kate shouted to Victor. She didn't see Paolo.

'You can't stop me,' Victor said.

'*I* can!' Paolo said from behind. Victor started to turn and Paolo hit him on the head with the bottle.

'Crash!'

That was Victor hitting the floor.

'Whoooomph!'

That was the fire.

'Quick, Paolo!' I shouted. 'In my lorry! There's a phone!'

That was six weeks ago. Paolo, Antonio and Victor were OK. The police took them, Kate and me to the police station. We told the police everything we knew. The next day Kate and I went back to the Web Café.

But Paolo didn't come with us. He helped the police and told them all about the Vassallo brothers. But he got six weeks in prison. The Vassallo brothers got ten years in prison.

I worked at the café while Paolo was in prison. Because I had no lorry, I had no job. I liked helping Kate, of course. But she wasn't happy because Paolo wasn't there.

Today Kate and I are happy because Paolo's back from prison. He got back to the café at twelve o'clock with a big smile on his face. We sat down at a table in the kitchen and had lunch – pizza! My last lunch at the café. Now that Paolo was back they did not need me.

After lunch Kate left the kitchen and came back with a pizza box.

'This is for you, Matt,' Kate said and gave me the box.

'Thank you, but I'm not hungry now,' I replied.

'Open it,' Kate said with a little smile.

I opened the box. But there wasn't a pizza in it. Just a piece of paper. There was some writing on the paper, but it wasn't in English.

'What does it say?' I asked, giving the paper to Paolo.

He laughed. 'It's in Maltese,' he replied. 'It says "Don't stop now!" We don't want you to go. We need you here in the café. You are in our family now.'

I looked at Paolo and Kate.

'Yes! Thank you!' I said with a big smile. And Kate put her arms around me and gave me a long kiss!

Cambridge English Readers

Look out for these other titles in the series:

Blood Diamonds
by Richard MacAndrew

Journalists Harley Kirkpatrick and Annie Shepherd think they have their biggest story: 'blood diamonds' from Africa. But do they know the danger they are now in?

The Big Picture
by Sue Leather

Ken Harada takes photos for newspapers. But life gets dangerous when Ken takes a photo of a sumo star. Someone wants the photo badly. But who? And why?

Bad Love
by Sue Leather

"Dr. Jack Daly?" Judy said. "He's famous."
"I often don't like famous people," I said.
"Oh come on, Detective Laine!"
  One week later Daly is dead and Flick Laine is looking for his killer.

Parallel
by Colin Campbell

'Max sat on his bed. There was a gun on the bed beside him. The gun was still warm.'
  Max kills for money. But one day he goes to a new world and changes his life.